Easy Steps
to Chinese
for Kids

轻松学中文

少儿版

Yamin Ma
Xinying Li

北京语言大学出版社
BEIJING LANGUAGE AND CULTURE
UNIVERSITY PRESS

图书在版编目（CIP）数据

轻松学中文：少儿版：英文版．1b．课本 ／ 马亚敏，李欣颖编著．
－北京：北京语言大学出版社，2011.8（2017.10 重印）
ISBN 978-7-5619-3048-9

Ⅰ．①轻… Ⅱ．①马…②李… Ⅲ．①汉语－对外汉语教学
－教材 Ⅳ．①H195.4

中国版本图书馆CIP数据核字（2011）第114830号

书　　名	**轻松学中文**（少儿版）英文版 课本 1b
	QINGSONG XUE ZHONGWEN (SHAO'ER BAN) YINGWEN BAN KEBEN 1b
责任编辑	王亚莉　孙玉婷
美术策划	王　宇
封面设计	王　宇　王章定
版式设计	北京鑫联必升文化发展有限公司
责任印制	汪学发
出版发行	北京语言大学出版社
社　　址	北京市海淀区学院路15号　邮政编码：100083
网　　址	www.blcup.com
电　　话	编辑部 8610－82303647/3592/3395
	国内发行部 8610－82303650/3591/3648/3653
	海外拓展部 8610－82300309/3365/0361/3080
网上订购	8610－82303908　service@blcup.com
印　　刷	北京联兴盛业印刷股份有限公司
经　　销	全国新华书店
版　　次	2011年8月第1版　2017年10月第8次印刷
开　　本	889mm×1194mm　1/16　印张：6.25
字　　数	35千字
书　　号	ISBN 978-7-5619-3048-9/H.11089
	07800

©2011 北京语言大学出版社

Easy Steps to Chinese for Kids (Textbook) 1b
Yamin Ma, Xinying Li

Editors	Yali Wang, Yuting Sun
Art design	Arthur Y. Wang
Cover design	Arthur Y. Wang, Zhangding Wang
Graphic design	Beijing XinLianBiSheng Cultural Development Co.,1td.

Published by
Beijing Language & Culture University Press
No.15 Xueyuan Road, Haidian District, Beijing, China 100083
Distributed by
Beijing Language & Culture University Press
No.15 Xueyuan Road, Haidian District, Beijing, China 100083
First published in September 2011
Printed in China
Copyright © 2011 Beijing Language & Culture University Press

Website: www.blcup.com

ACKNOWLEDGEMENTS

A number of people have helped us to put the books into publication. Particular thanks are owed to the following:

- 戚德祥先生、张健女士、苗强先生 who trusted our expertise in the field of Chinese language teaching and learning

- Editors 王亚莉女士、唐琪佳女士、黄英女士、孙玉婷女士 for their meticulous work

- Graphic designers 王章定先生、李越女士 for their artistic design for the cover and content

- Art consultant Arthur Y. Wang for his professional guidance and artists 陆颖女士、孙颉先生、陈丽女士 for their artistic ability in beautiful illustration

- 范明女士、徐景瑄、左佳侬、田沐子、南珊、陈子钰 who helped with the sound recordings and 徐景瑄 for his proofreading work

- 刘慧 who helped with the song recordings

- Chinese teachers from the kindergarten section and Heads of the Chinese Department of Xavier School 李京燕女士、余莉莉女士 for their helpful advice and encouragement

- And finally, members of our families who have always given us generous support

INTRODUCTION

- The primary goal of this series *Easy Steps to Chinese for Kids* is to help total beginners, particularly children from a non-Chinese background, build a solid foundation for learning Chinese as a foreign language.
- The series is designed to emphasize the development of communication skills in listening and speaking. Recognizing characters and writing characters are also the focus of this series.
- This series employs the Communicative Approach, and also takes into account the unique characteristics of the children when they engage in language learning at an early age.
- Each lesson has a song using all the new words and sentences.
- Chinese culture is introduced in a fun way.
- This series consists of 8 colour books, which cover 4 levels. Each level has 2 colour books (a and b).
- Each textbook contains a CD of new words, texts, listening exercises, *pinyin* and songs, and is supplemented by a workbook, word cards, picture flashcards and a CD-ROM.

COURSE DESIGN

- **Character** writing is introduced in a step-by-step fashion, starting with strokes, radicals and simple characters.
- *Pinyin* is not formally introduced until Book 3a, as we believe that too-early exposure to *pinyin* will confuse children who are also learning to read and write in their mother tongue.
- **Language skills in listening and speaking** are the emphasis of this series, and the language materials are carefully selected and relevant to children of this age group.
- **Motor skills** will be developed through all kinds

简介

- 《轻松学中文》（少儿版）旨在帮助那些母语为非汉语的初学儿童奠定扎实的汉语学习基础。
- 本套教材的目标是通过强调在听、说能力方面的训练来培养语言交流技能。同时，识字和书写汉字也是这套系列教材的重点。
- 教材中采用了交际法，并在课程设计中考虑到儿童在这个特定的年龄段学外语的特点。
- 每课配有一首歌曲，用歌曲的形式把当课的生词和句子唱出来。
- 中国文化的介绍是通过趣味性的活动来实现的。
- 本套教材分为四级，每级分为a、b两本彩色课本，共8本。
- 每本课本后附有一张CD，录有生词、课文、听力练习、拼音和歌曲。课本还另配练习册、词语卡片、图卡和CD-ROM光盘。

课程设计

- 汉字书写先从笔画、偏旁部首和简单汉字着手。
- 拼音从3a才开始系统介绍，因为小朋友过早学拼音可能会影响他们母语的阅读和书写能力的培养。
- 听、说技能的培养是本套教材的重点，所选语料适合小朋友的年龄段及其兴趣爱好。
- 小朋友的手部握笔掌控能力的培养是通过各种精心设计的有趣活动来实现的，这些活动可以是画线、画图、上色、描红、做手工等。
- 认知能力的培养是儿童早期教育的一个重点。

of fun and interesting activities, including drawing lines and pictures, colouring, tracing characters and making handicrafts, etc.

- **Cognitive ability** is a very important aspect of early schooling. By understanding the world around them through shapes, colours, directions, etc., children may find Chinese language learning more exciting, fun and relevant.

- **Logical thinking and imaginative skills** are nurtured through a variety of activities and practice, which create space for children to develop these skills as early as possible.

- **A variety of activities,** such as songs, games, handworks, etc., are carefully designed to motivate the children to learn.

- **Hands-on practice** is carefully designed throughout the series to make learning meaningful and enhance retention.

- **The pace** for developing language knowledge and skills takes a gradual approach, which makes it easy for children to build a solid foundation for learning Chinese.

通过图形、颜色、方向的学习，小朋友认识了他们周边的世界，汉语学习也变得活泼、有趣，小朋友还能活学活用。

- 通过一系列精心设计的活动和练习，培养小朋友的逻辑思维和想象力。

- 各种各样、丰富多彩的活动，比如歌曲、游戏、手工等，都是为了激发小朋友学习汉语的积极性。

- 动手能力的练习贯穿始终，使小朋友学起来更有意思，也有助于他们掌握和巩固新学的内容。

- 学习的节奏由慢到快，循序渐进，使小朋友轻松打好汉语学习的基础。

COURSE LENGTH

课程进度

- This series is designed for young children or primary school students.

- With one lesson daily, primary school students can complete learning one level, i.e. two books, within an academic year.

- Once all the eight books have been completed, learners can move onto the series *Easy Steps to Chinese* (Books 1-8), which is designed for teenagers from a non-Chinese background.

- As this series is continuous and ongoing, each book can be taught within any time span according to the students' levels of Chinese proficiency.

- 本套教材专为幼儿或小学生编写。

- 如果每天都有汉语课，大部分学生可以在一年内学完一个级别的两本。

- 如果学完四级8本，学生可以继续学习同一系列的为非华裔中学生编写的《轻松学中文》（1—8册）。

- 由于本教材的内容是连贯的，教师可根据学生的水平来决定教学进度。

HOW TO USE THIS BOOK

①

New words are introduced through pictures.

②

The children are encouraged to say the new words correctly and memorize their meanings using different ways.

③

The texts are presented in forms of phrases, sentences or dialogues.

④

The songs will help the children memorize the new words and sentences in a fun way.

The children develop their speaking skills through picture talks.

⑤

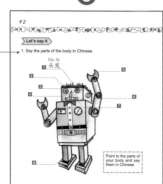

⑥

The children learn to write strokes, which is the basic training for writing characters later on.

7

Fun activities are designed to reinforce and consolidate language learning.

8

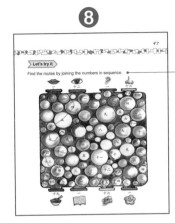

Such activities provide opportunities for the children to develop their logical thinking and imagination.

9

Such exercises are designed for the children to practise their character writing.

10

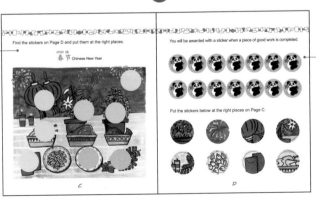

This section of Chinese culture can be introduced whenever the need arises.

Stickers are given to the children when a good piece of work is completed.

CONTENTS 目 录

第一课 爸爸、妈妈

①

bà ba

爸爸
dad

②

mā ma

妈妈
mum

③

ài

爱
love;
like

Let's practise

Fill in the boxes with the words given. Write down the letters.

1) 我 ^{wǒ} ☐e 爸爸、妈妈。 ^{bà ba} ^{mā ma}

5) 我五 ^{wǒ wǔ} ☐ 。

2) 你 ^{nǐ} ☐ ！

6) 我 ^{wǒ} ☐ 一年级。 ^{yī nián jí}

3) 再 ^{zài} ☐ ！

7) 谢谢 ^{xiè xie} ☐ ！

4) 我 ^{wǒ} ☐ 京京。 ^{jīng jing}

8) ☐ 客气。 ^{kè qi}

a) 你 ^{nǐ}   b) 好 ^{hǎo}   c) 见 ^{jiàn}   d) 不 ^{bù}

e) 爱 ^{ài}   f) 岁 ^{suì}   g) 上 ^{shàng}   h) 叫 ^{jiào}

Let's use new words 02

①

bà ba　　mā ma
爸爸、妈妈

ài　wǒ
爱我。

②

wǒ ài bà ba
我爱爸爸。

wǒ ài mā ma
我爱妈妈。

Let's sing 　◎03　🖊　我爱爸爸、妈妈

♩ = 90

爸爸、妈 妈 爱 我 , 我 爱 爸 爸、妈

妈 。爸爸、妈 妈 爱 我 , 我 爱 爸爸、妈 妈 。

Let's say it

Complete the conversations.

①
nǐ jiào shén me míng zi
你叫什么名字?

②
nín zǎo
您早!

③
zài jiàn
再见!

④
nín hǎo
您好!

> **Let's write**

1. Learn the strokes.

héng zhé wān gōu

①

shù wān gōu

②

2. Trace the strokes.

①

héng zhé wān gōu	héng zhé wān gōu	héng zhé wān gōu
九 九	九 九	九 九

héng zhé wān gōu	héng zhé wān gōu	héng zhé wān gōu
九 九	九 九	九 九

②

shù wān gōu	shù wān gōu	shù wān gōu
七 七	七 七	七 七

shù wān gōu	shù wān gōu	shù wān gōu
七 七	七 七	七 七

> Let's play

INSTRUCTION

Each child is given a card with one stroke on it. When the teacher shows the class a character, the children should match the strokes on the cards they are holding with the character in the teacher's hands.

Some examples:

liù	shí	dà	mù
六	十	大	木

qī	tiān	bā	wǔ
七	天	八	五

xiǎo	shǎo	bù	
小	少	不	

Let's try it

Colour in the shapes with the colours given. Count up and say the numbers in Chinese.

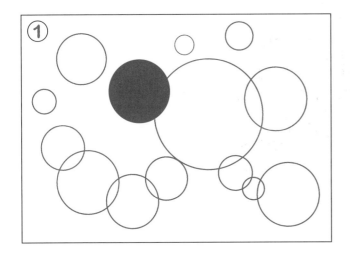

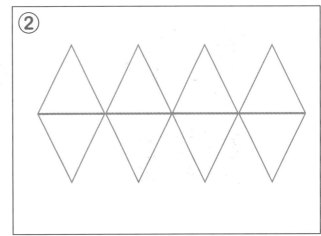

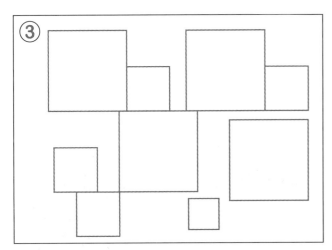

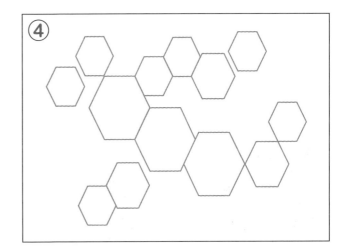

 14

It's time to work

1. Match the pictures with the Chinese.

bà ba
爸爸

mā ma
妈妈

2. Match the pictures above with the ones below when they were children.

3. Draw pictures of your mum and dad.

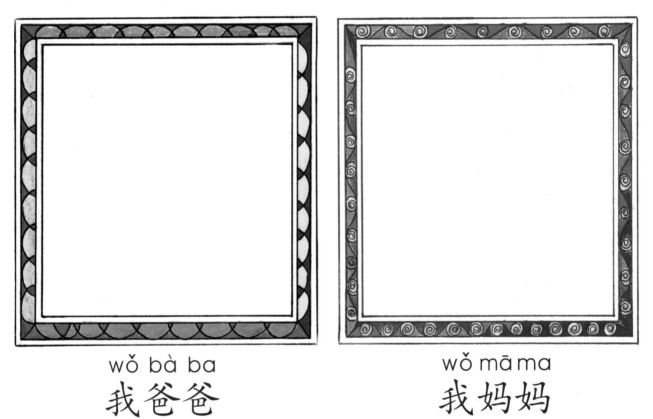

wǒ bà ba
我爸爸

wǒ mā ma
我妈妈

4. Write the strokes.

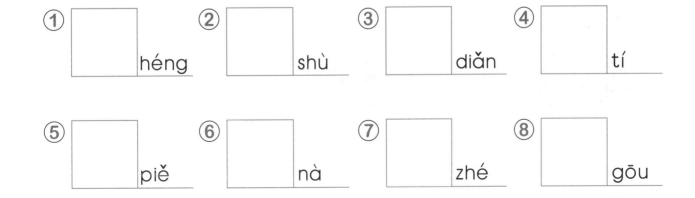

① héng ② shù ③ diǎn ④ tí

⑤ piě ⑥ nà ⑦ zhé ⑧ gōu

第二课 哥哥、姐姐

> **Let's learn new words** 04

①
gē ge
哥哥
elder brother

②
jiě jie
姐姐
elder sister

③
dì di
弟弟 younger brother

④
mèimei
妹妹 younger sister

⑤
yǒu
有 have

> **Let's practise**

Complete the sentences with the Chinese given.

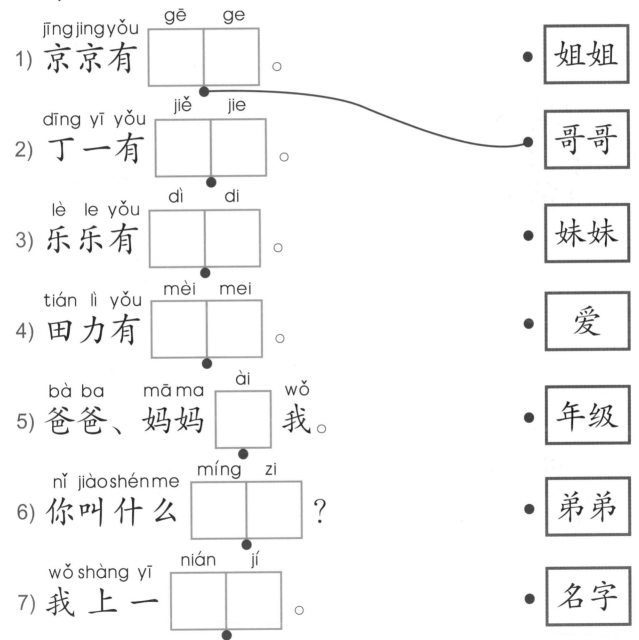

Let's use new words 05

京京

① wǒ yǒu gē ge
我有哥哥。

丁一

② wǒ yǒu jiě jie
我有姐姐。

③ wǒ yǒu dì di
我有弟弟。

田力

乐乐

④ wǒ yǒu mèi mei
我有妹妹。

Let's sing   我有哥哥

♩ = 50

哥哥、姐姐、弟弟、妹妹，哥哥、姐姐、弟弟、妹妹。

我有哥哥，我有姐姐，我有弟弟，我有妹妹。

Let's say it

Say one sentence for each picture.

哥哥

京京

EXAMPLE

jīng jing yǒu gē ge
京京有哥哥。

姐姐

弟弟

弟弟

丁一

①

②

田力

妹妹

弟弟

③

哥哥

弟弟

乐乐

Draw a picture of your family and say one sentence about it.

> **Let's write**

1. Learn the strokes.

piě zhé

①  么

wān gōu

② 字

2. Trace the strokes.

①

piě zhé	piě zhé	piě zhé
么 么	么 么	么 么
piě zhé	piě zhé	piě zhé
么 么	么 么	么 么

②

wān gōu	wān gōu	wān gōu
字 字	字 字	字 字
wān gōu	wān gōu	wān gōu
字 字	字 字	字 字

nǐ jiào shén me míng zi
你叫什么名字？

Let's play

INSTRUCTION

The class is divided into small groups. The teacher whispers a sentence to one member of each group. The sentence is whispered along to the last child who is expected to say it correctly. If the last child does not say the sentence correctly, this group is out of the game.

Some examples:

nǐ jiào shén me míng zi
1) 你叫什么名字？

lǎo shī nín hǎo
2) 老师，您好！

wǒ shàng yī nián jí
3) 我上一年级。

bà ba mā ma ài wǒ
4) 爸爸、妈妈爱我。

wǒ yǒu gē ge
5) 我有哥哥。

> **Let's try it**

Colour in their hair.

①

②

③

④

It's time to work

1. Find their brothers and sisters.

①
tián lì yǒu mèimei
田力有妹妹。

③
jīng jing yǒu gē ge
京京有哥哥。

②
dīng yī yǒu jiě jie
丁一有姐姐。

④
lè le yǒu dì di
乐乐有弟弟。

2. Write the strokes that each character has.

① me

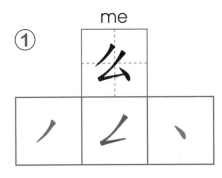

② xiǎo

小

③ dà

大

④ qiān

千

⑤ kǒu

口

⑥ jiǔ

九

⑦ qī

七

⑧ shǒu

手

Let's learn new words

  07

①
wǒ de
我的
my

②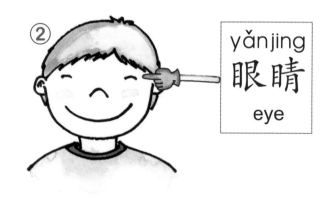
yǎn jing
眼睛
eye

③
bí zi
鼻子
nose

④
zuǐ ba
嘴巴
mouth

⑤
ěr duo
耳朵
ear

Let's practise

Say the parts of the body in Chinese.

EXAMPLE

yǎnjing
眼睛

① ② ③ ④ ⑤ ⑥ ⑦

Let's use new words 08

①

wǒ de yǎnjing
我的眼睛

京京

②

wǒ de bí zi
我的鼻子

丁一

④

wǒ de ěr duo
我的耳朵

乐乐

③

wǒ de zuǐ ba
我的嘴巴

田力

Let's sing　09　🖊　我的眼睛

♩ = 48

眼 睛、鼻 子、嘴 巴、耳 朵,眼 睛、鼻 子、嘴 巴、耳 朵。

我 的 眼 睛,我 的 鼻 子,我 的 嘴 巴、耳 朵。

Let's say it

1. Say the parts of the body in Chinese by following the example.

EXAMPLE

① wǒ de yǎnjing
我 的 眼 睛

② wǒ de ěr duo
我 的 耳 朵

③ wǒ de bí zi
我 的 鼻 子

④ wǒ de zuǐ ba
我 的 嘴 巴

Draw a picture of yourself.

2. Colour in the parts of the body and say them in Chinese.

①

yǎn jing

眼睛

②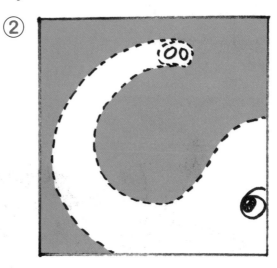

bí zi

鼻子

③

ěr duo

耳朵

④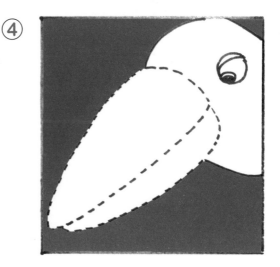

zuǐ ba

嘴巴

Let's write

1. Learn the strokes.

xié gōu

① 我

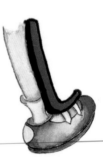

shù zhé zhé gōu

② 弟

2. Trace the strokes.

①

xié gōu	xié gōu	xié gōu
我 我	我 我	我 我

xié gōu	xié gōu	xié gōu
我 我	我 我	我 我

②

shù zhé zhé gōu	shù zhé zhé gōu	shù zhé zhé gōu
弟 弟	弟 弟	弟 弟

shù zhé zhé gōu	shù zhé zhé gōu	shù zhé zhé gōu
弟 弟	弟 弟	弟 弟

Let's play

bí zi
鼻子

INSTRUCTION
When the teacher says a part of the body, every child is expected to point to the right part. Those who point to a wrong part are out of the game.

Some examples:

bí zi
鼻子

yǎn jing
眼睛

zuǐ ba
嘴巴

ěr duo
耳朵

Let's try it

Match each part of the body with the right picture.

① yǎn jing 眼睛

② bí zi 鼻子

③ zuǐ ba 嘴巴

④ ěr duo 耳朵

⑤ zuǐ ba 嘴巴

⑥ ěr duo 耳朵

It's time to work

1. Match the parts of the body with the Chinese.

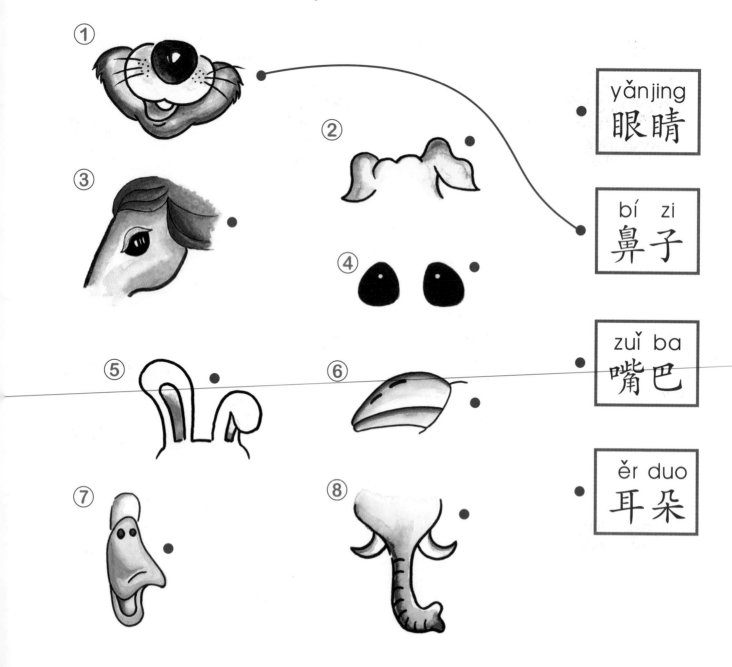

2. Find the strokes and trace them with the colours given.

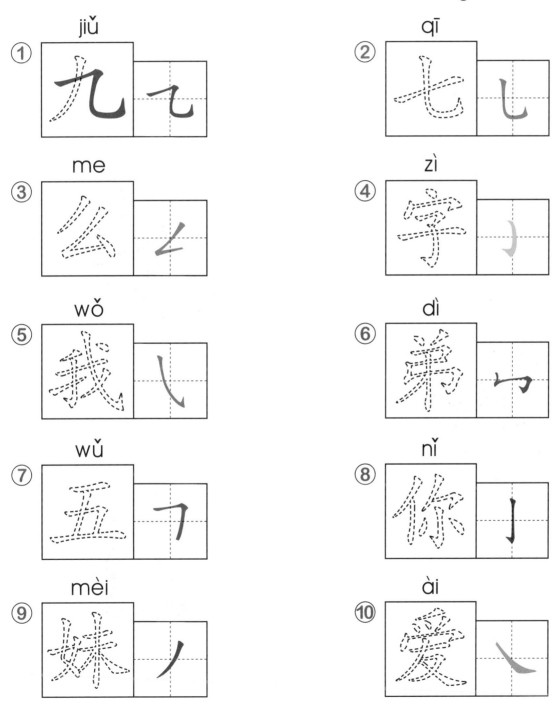

① jiǔ

② qī

③ me

④ zì

⑤ wǒ

⑥ dì

⑦ wǔ

⑧ nǐ

⑨ mèi

⑩ ài

第四课 头和手

> **Let's learn new words** 10 🖊

①
tóu
头
head

②
tóu fa
头发
hair

③
shǒu
手
hand

④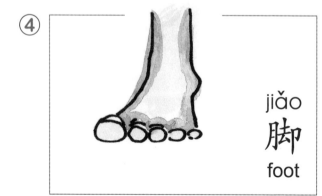
jiǎo
脚
foot

Let's practise

Match the parts of the body with the Chinese.

a
tóu
头

b
shǒu
手

c
jiǎo
脚

d
tóu fa
头发

e
ěr duo
耳朵

f
bí zi
鼻子

h
yǎn jing
眼睛

g
zuǐ ba
嘴巴

Let's use new words

11

①

wǒ de tóu
我的头

京京

②

wǒ de tóu fa
我的头发

丁一

③

wǒ de shǒu
我的 手

田力

④

乐乐

wǒ de jiǎo
我的脚

Let's sing  我的手和脚

我 的 头、头　发，我 的 手 和 脚，

hé
and

我 的 头、头　发，我 的 手 和 脚。

1. Say the parts of the body in Chinese.

tóu fa
头发

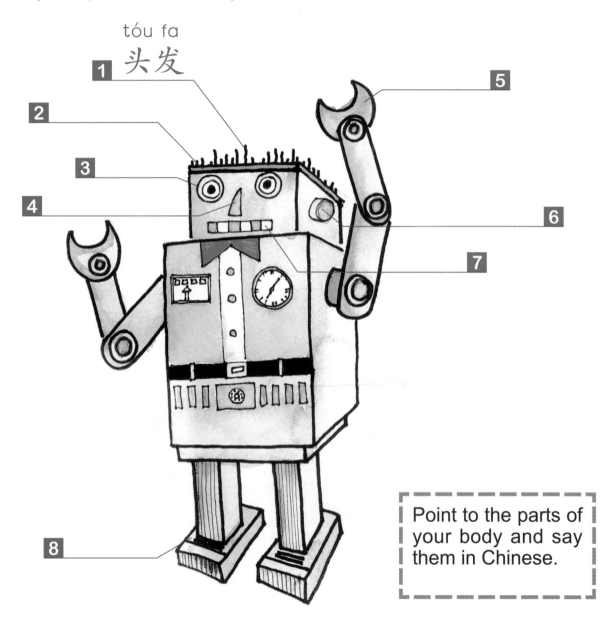

Point to the parts of your body and say them in Chinese.

2. Circle the wrong parts of the body and say them in Chinese.

EXAMPLE

tóu
头

Let's write

1. Learn the strokes.

héng zhé gōu

① 有

piě diǎn

② 姐

2. Trace the strokes.

①

héng zhé gōu	héng zhé gōu	héng zhé gōu
有 有	有 有	有 有
héng zhé gōu	héng zhé gōu	héng zhé gōu
有 有	有 有	有 有

②

piě diǎn	piě diǎn	piě diǎn
姐 姐	姐 姐	姐 姐
piě diǎn	piě diǎn	piě diǎn
姐 姐	姐 姐	姐 姐

bí zi
鼻子

Let's play

INSTRUCTION

When the teacher says a part of the body, every child is expected to point to the right part. Those who point to a wrong part are out of the game.

Some examples:

bí zi	yǎn jing	zuǐ ba	ěr duo
鼻子	眼睛	嘴巴	耳朵

tóu	tóu fa	shǒu	jiǎo
头	头发	手	脚

Let's try it

Find the routes by joining the numbers in sequence.

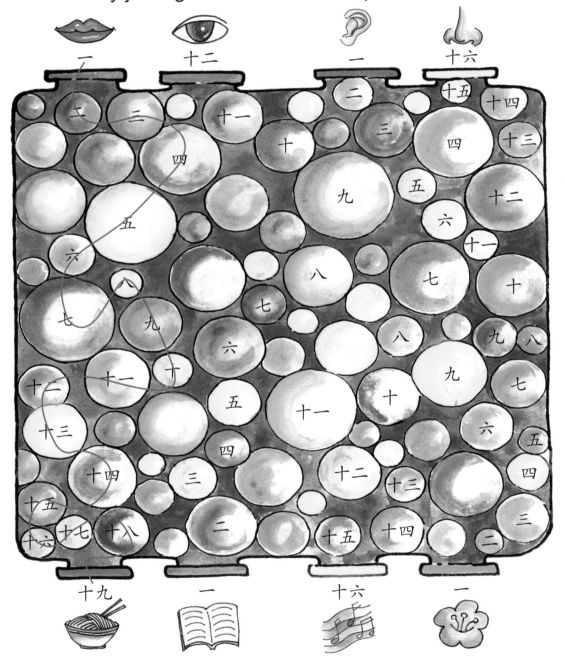

It's time to work

1. Match the parts of a character with the full character.

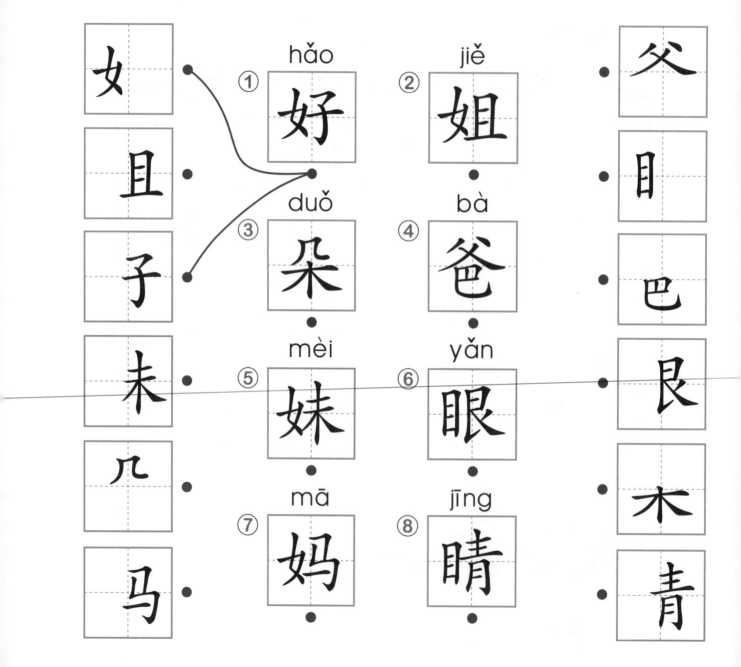

2. Find the strokes and trace them with the colours given.

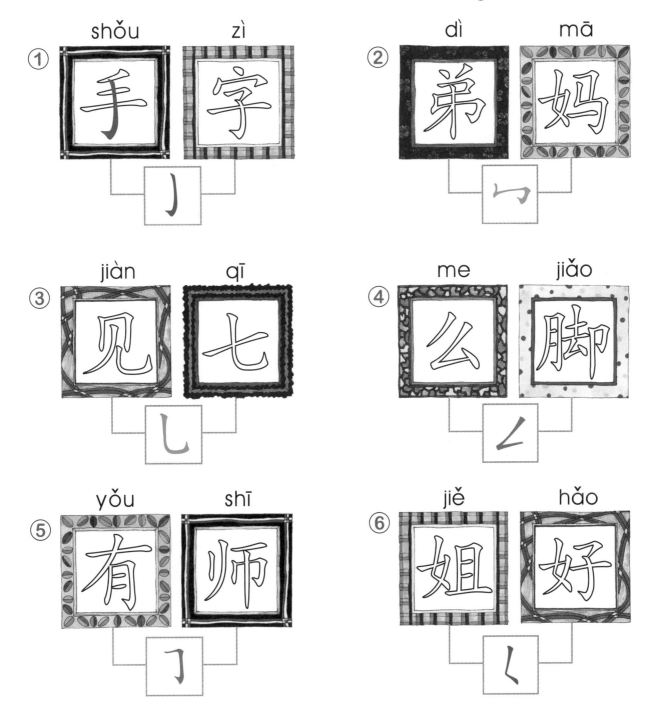

第五课 猫和狗

> Let's learn new words 13

① xǐ huan
喜 欢
like

② māo
猫
cat

③ gǒu
狗
dog

④ wū guī
乌龟
turtle

⑤ jīn yú
金鱼
goldfish

Let's practise

Say the parts of the body in Chinese.

jīn yú de tóu
金鱼的头 1
's; of

①  乐乐

wǒ xǐ huan māo

我喜欢猫。

②  京京

wǒ xǐ huan gǒu

我喜欢狗。

③  丁一

wǒ xǐ huan wū guī

我喜欢乌龟。

④  田力

wǒ xǐ huan jīn yú

我喜欢金鱼。

Let's sing   15   我喜欢乌龟

♩ = 46

xiǎo
你喜欢小猫 和小狗, 我喜欢乌龟 和金鱼。
small; little

你喜欢小猫 和小狗, 我喜欢乌龟 和金鱼。

Let's say it

1. Match the Chinese with the right boxes and say the parts of the
   body in Chinese.

① tóu
头

② shǒu
手

③ jiǎo
脚

④ tóu fa
头发

⑤ ěr duo
耳朵

⑥ bí zi
鼻子

⑧ yǎn jing
眼睛

⑦ zuǐ ba
嘴巴

2. Say the parts of the body in Chinese.

lè le de tóu
乐乐的头

1

2

3

4

5

6

7

8

Describe yourself by following the example.

Let's write

1. Learn the strokes.

héng zhé zhé piě

①  级

wò gōu

② 您

2. Trace the strokes.

①
héng zhé zhé piě	héng zhé zhé piě	héng zhé zhé piě
级 级	级 级	级 级
héng zhé zhé piě	héng zhé zhé piě	héng zhé zhé piě
级 级	级 级	级 级

②
wò gōu	wò gōu	wò gōu
您 您	您 您	您 您
wò gōu	wò gōu	wò gōu
您 您	您 您	您 您

> **Let's play**

INSTRUCTION

One child is shown a card with a Chinese word on it. The child is asked to draw a picture to illustrate the meaning of the word, and the rest of the class are expected to say the word out loud in Chinese after seeing the picture.

wū guī
乌龟

Some examples:

wū guī	māo	gǒu	jīn yú	shǒu	jiǎo
乌龟	猫	狗	金鱼	手	脚

bí zi	zuǐ ba	tóu	tóu fa
鼻子	嘴巴	头	头发

> **Let's try it**

Match the Chinese with the pictures.

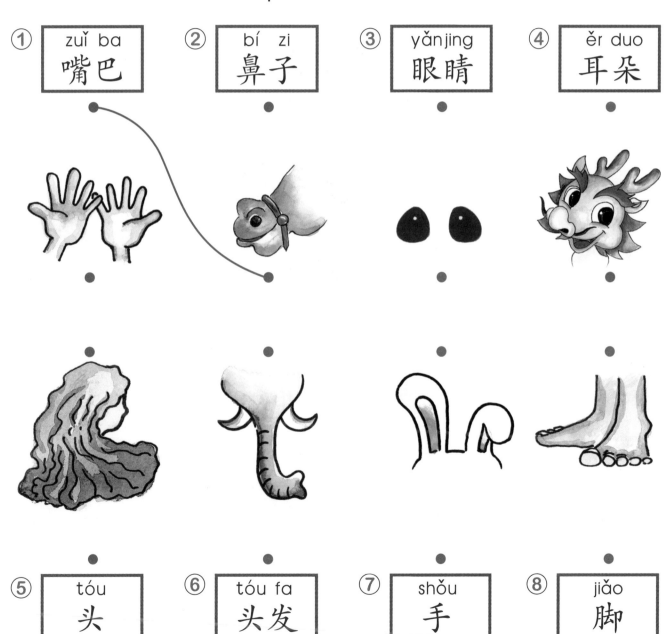

① zuǐ ba 嘴巴

② bí zi 鼻子

③ yǎn jing 眼睛

④ ěr duo 耳朵

⑤ tóu 头

⑥ tóu fa 头发

⑦ shǒu 手

⑧ jiǎo 脚

> **It's time to work**

1. Match the Chinese with the pictures.

① māo de yǎn jing
猫 的 眼睛

② gǒu de zuǐ ba
狗 的 嘴巴

③ wū guī de jiǎo
乌龟 的 脚

④ jīn yú de tóu
金鱼 的 头

⑤ jīng jing de shǒu
京京 的 手

⑥ lè le de tóu fa
乐乐 的 头发

⑦ tián lì de bí zi
田力 的 鼻子

⑧ dīng yī de ěr duo
丁一 的 耳朵

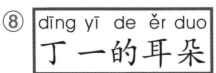

2. Fill in the brackets with the missing buttons.

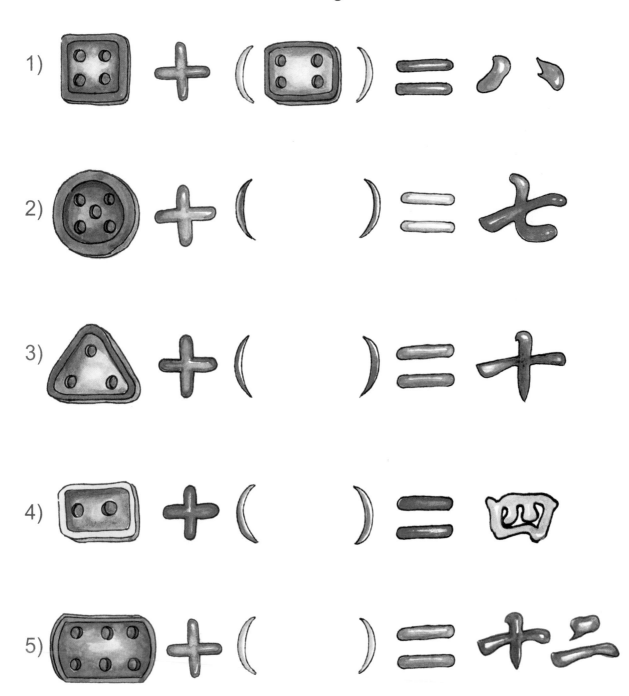

第六课 红色、蓝色

Let's learn new words 🎧 16 ✏️

① hóng sè
红 色
red

② huáng sè
黄 色
yellow

③ lán sè
蓝色
blue

④ lǜ sè
绿色
green

> Let's practise

Read aloud and say the meaning of each word.

EXAMPLE

hóng sè 红色	hóng sè **red**

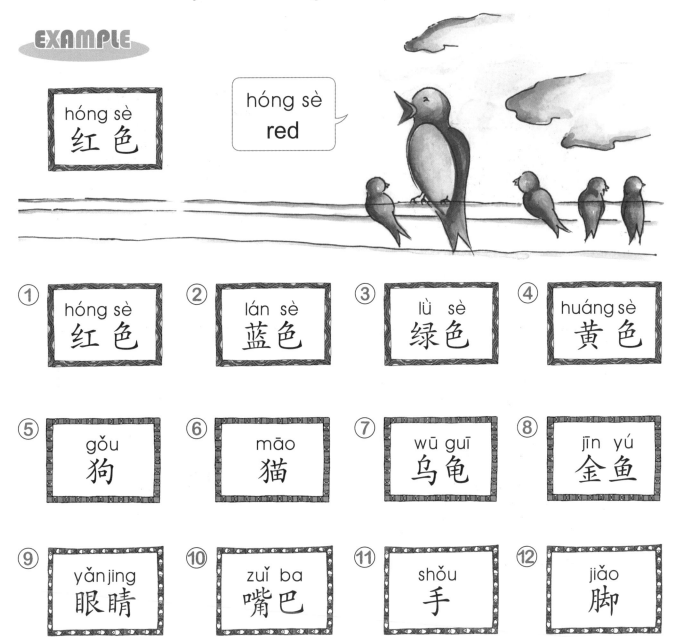

① hóng sè 红色

② lán sè 蓝色

③ lǜ sè 绿色

④ huáng sè 黄色

⑤ gǒu 狗

⑥ māo 猫

⑦ wū guī 乌龟

⑧ jīn yú 金鱼

⑨ yǎn jing 眼睛

⑩ zuǐ ba 嘴巴

⑪ shǒu 手

⑫ jiǎo 脚

64

Let's use new words   17

①

dīng yī xǐ huan hóng sè
丁一喜欢红色。

②

lè le xǐ huan huáng sè
乐乐喜欢黄色。

③

tián lì xǐ huan lán sè
田力喜欢蓝色。

④

jīng jing xǐ huan lù sè
京京喜欢绿色。

Let's sing 18 我喜欢绿色

♩ = 62

1. 你 喜欢 红 色， 喜欢蓝 色。
2. 你 喜欢 红 色， 喜欢蓝 色。

我 喜欢 绿 色， 喜欢黄 色。
我 喜欢 绿 色， 喜欢黄 色。

Let's say it

Find the items of the same shape and colour them in. Count up and say the numbers in Chinese.

Let's write

1. Learn the strokes.

héng piě

①  名

shù wān

② 四

2. Trace the strokes.

①

héng piě	héng piě	héng piě
名 名	名 名	名 名

héng piě	héng piě	héng piě
名 名	名 名	名 名

②

shù wān	shù wān	shù wān
四 四	四 四	四 四

shù wān	shù wān	shù wān
四 四	四 四	四 四

> **Let's play**

hóng sè
红色

INSTRUCTION

The teacher says a colour in Chinese, and the children are expected to find an item of that colour in the classroom and touch it. The children should be encouraged to find as many items of that colour as possible.

Some examples:

hóng sè	huáng sè	lán sè	lǜ sè
红色	黄色	蓝色	绿色

Let's try it

Colour in the buttons with the colours given.

two-hole button
hóng sè
红色

three-hole button
huáng sè
黄色

four-hole button
lǜ sè
绿色

five-hole button
lán sè
蓝色

It's time to work

Join the numbers in sequence and colour in the picture.

2. Find the strokes and trace them with the colours given.

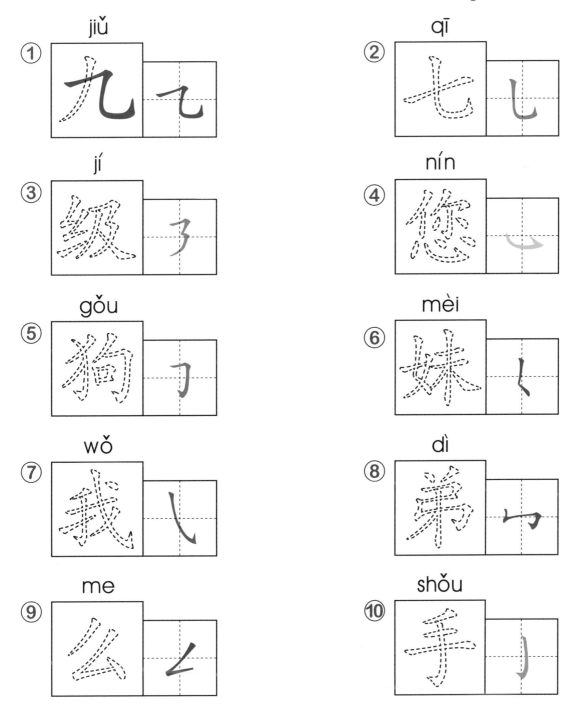

第七课 苹果、香蕉

①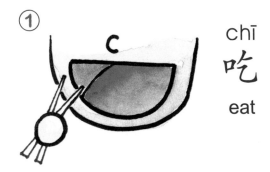
chī
吃
eat

②
píngguǒ
苹果
apple

③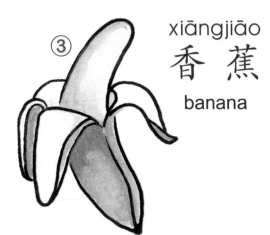
xiāngjiāo
香蕉
banana

④
cǎoméi
草莓
strawberry

⑤
pú tao
葡萄
grape

Let's practise

Describe the pictures by following the example.

EXAMPLE

lǜ sè de píngguǒ
绿色的苹果

①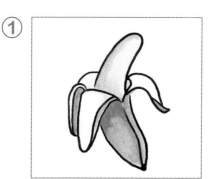

②

③

④

⑤

⑥

⑦

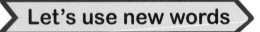

Let's use new words 20

① wǒ ài chī píng guǒ
我爱吃苹果。

② wǒ ài chī xiāng jiāo
我爱吃香蕉。

③ wǒ ài chī cǎo méi
我爱吃草莓。

④ wǒ ài chī pú tao
我爱吃葡萄。

Let's sing ◉21 ✎ 苹果、苹果，我爱吃

♩= 48

苹 果、苹 果，我 爱 吃。香 蕉、香 蕉，我 爱 吃。

草莓、草莓，我爱吃。葡萄、葡萄，我 爱 吃。

Let's say it

1. Find the pictures for each colour
   and say the numbers in Chinese.

hóng sè 红色	❷	⑫
huáng sè 黄色		
lán sè 蓝色		
lù sè 绿色		

2. Describe the animals and fruit
   you have learned.

EXAMPLE

hóng sè de māo
红 色 的 猫

Let's write

1. Learn the strokes.

héng gōu

① 你

shù tí

② 眼

2. Trace the strokes.

①

héng gōu	héng gōu	héng gōu
你 你	你 你	你 你
héng gōu	héng gōu	héng gōu
你 你	你 你	你 你

②

shù tí	shù tí	shù tí
眼 眼	眼 眼	眼 眼
shù tí	shù tí	shù tí
眼 眼	眼 眼	眼 眼

> Let's play

Count up and say the numbers in Chinese.

hóng píngguǒ	lǜ píngguǒ	lǜ pú tao	huáng xiāng jiāo	hóng cǎoméi
红苹果	绿苹果	绿葡萄	黄香蕉	红草莓
12				

Let's try it

Join the numbers from "一" to "二十" to help each animal find its food.

一	十一	二	五	一	六	七	一	四	一	十
三	十二	四	三	二	五	八	二	三	二	九
四	十三	五	六	七	七	六	五	四	三	四
五	十一	十	九	八	八	九	十	十一	六	五
六	十二	十三	十四	十五	九	十四	十三	十二	七	八
七	八	九	十	十六	十四	十五	十二	十一	十	九
十四	十三	十二	十一	十七	十三	十六	十三	十九	十七	十八
十五	十六	十七	十八	十八	十九	十七	十四	十五	十六	十九
十六	十七	二十	十九	十七	二十	十八	十九	二十	十七	二十

It's time to work

1. Match each sentence with the right picture.

lè le xǐ huan lán sè   lǜ sè
乐乐喜欢蓝色、绿色。

jīng jing xǐ huan māo   gǒu
京京喜欢猫、狗。

dīng yī xǐ huan wū guī   jīn yú
丁一喜欢乌龟、金鱼。

tián lì xǐ huan chī píngguǒ
田力喜欢吃苹果。

2. Match the Chinese with the pictures and colour in the pictures with the colours given.

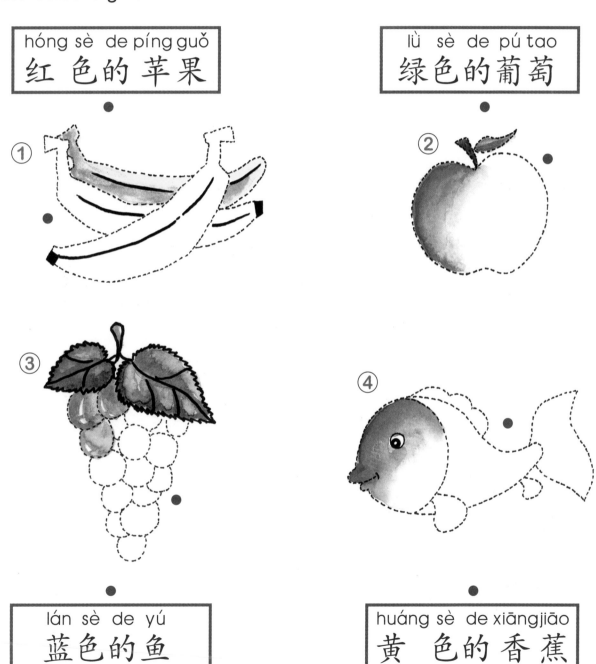

hóng sè de píng guǒ
红色的苹果

lǜ sè de pú tao
绿色的葡萄

① ②

③ ④

lán sè de yú
蓝色的鱼

huáng sè de xiāng jiāo
黄色的香蕉

中国文化 Chinese Culture

chūn jié
春节

Chinese New Year

Chinese New Year is the most important festival for the Chinese people. It falls on the first day of the first month in the Chinese lunar calendar. On the New Year's Eve, every family gathers to eat a special dinner. They usually eat meat, chicken, fish, New Year cakes and dumplings, etc. On the first day of the Chinese New Year, people light firecrackers and children get red packets containing money. During the Chinese New Year, red colour is usually used for good luck.

A

Colour in the pictures.

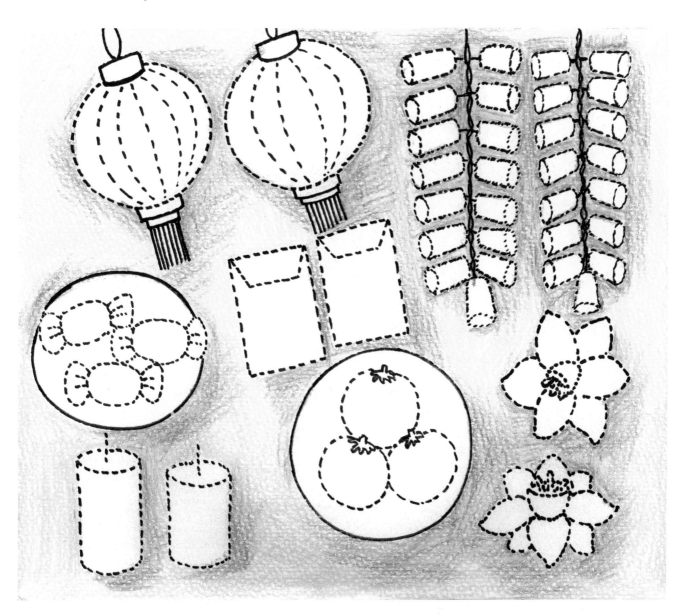

B

Find the stickers on Page D and put them at the right places.

chūn jié
春节 Chinese New Year

C

You will be awarded with a sticker when a piece of good work is completed.

Put the stickers below at the right places on Page C.

D

词汇表 VOCABULARY

Lesson 1

爸爸	bàba	dad
妈妈	māma	mum
爱	ài	love; like

Lesson 2

哥哥	gēge	elder brother
姐姐	jiějie	elder sister
弟弟	dìdi	younger brother
妹妹	mèimei	younger sister
有	yǒu	have

Lesson 3

我的	wǒ de	my
眼睛	yǎnjing	eye
鼻子	bízi	nose
嘴巴	zuǐba	mouth
耳朵	ěrduo	ear

Lesson 4

头	tóu	head
头发	tóufa	hair
手	shǒu	hand
脚	jiǎo	foot
○ 和	hé	and

Lesson 5

喜欢	xǐhuan	like
猫	māo	cat
狗	gǒu	dog
乌龟	wūguī	turtle
金鱼	jīnyú	goldfish
○ 的	de	's; of
○ 小	xiǎo	small; little

Lesson 6

红色	hóngsè	red
黄色	huángsè	yellow
蓝色	lánsè	blue
绿色	lǜsè	green

Lesson 7

吃	chī	eat
苹果	píngguǒ	apple
香蕉	xiāngjiāo	banana
草莓	cǎoméi	strawberry
葡萄	pútao	grape